Introduction by W. Terrence Gordon

In this unique essay, McLuhan comments, at the invitation of the editor, on nine contributions to *New Literary History*, Vol. II, No. 3; Spring, 1971. Pages 517– 531. His range of themes compels the reader to ride an intellectual *tsunami*, but these pages are also marked by a subtlety all but unmatched elsewhere in McLuhan's output. So, the "stranger" alluded to on the opening page, Plato's Eleatic Stranger, is linked to the theme of formal causality, explored so extensively in other key publications from McLuhan's pen. A reference to Aristotle hints at a source for McLuhan's development of the reversal principle as one of the laws of media. James Joyce's observations on the effect of mirrors invites a comparison with the reflecting pool in the myth of Narcissus. McLuhan cannot resist the occasion to integrate a commentary on television ("There is, as it were, an 'angelic' dimension in electric media, lacking even to the movie.") But for the most part, the scope and the sweep of his commentary is confined to literature, with little suasion but much suggestion that literary analysis may be approached as an application of the principle that the medium is the message: "The moment of metamorphosis is the moment of frustration, arrest, the hang-up. This moment can be realized dramatically in an [a]llusion, a parenthesis, an aside, or a sub-plot parallel to the larger action. The interface generated in these intervals is itself the occasion of metamorphosis and transformation of awareness." There are arresting comments on the Symbolists (Mallarmé in thrall to visual assumptions) and the theatre of the absurd (who but McLuhan could speak of the "poetic fun" of *Waiting for Godot?*) As for the theatrical elements named in the title, McLuhan moves the reader toward the conclusion that the mask, whether in the guise of the book, the newspaper, or television, is the message. – WTG

Roles, Masks and Performances

Marshall McLuhan

While puzzling over my role as commentator on this issue of *New Literary History*, I have tried to see the magazine itself as *performance*. A literary magazine exists to enhance community values among its readers. There is a sense in which a magazine is a vortex of energy, a mask which the reader puts on in order to perceive a field of action that would otherwise be outside his ken. If a reader must put on a magazine as a mask or a pattern of energy in order to organize his perceptions, the contributors must also put on the public created by the magazine, creating a reciprocal and complementary action. It is especially difficult for me as an outside commentator to focus both aspects of this process simultaneously. Perhaps I will be permitted the role of "the stranger" used by Plato to promote the ends of dialogue and to avoid the specialist exchanges of an "in-group."

The function of "the stranger" as the trigger for dialogue appears even in the self-appointed role of cab-drivers as philosophers. There is usually a stranger in the back seat. It is likely that if the passenger in a cab were another cab-driver, both would tend to gossip about familiar matters. Such, for example, is the manner of committees. If, however, every member of a committee were to table his ignorance instead of his expertise, there could be no gossip. Dialogue demands ignorance as a resource and a spur to exploration.

At a panel discussion on "Theatre and the Visual Arts" with W. H. Auden and Buckminster Fuller, I ventured to ask what effect, if any, Apollo 14 might have on the theatre of the present and future. Auden proclaimed: "I am a nineteenth-century man and proud if it!" This comes to mind as I turn to the "Poetics of Spectacle" by Stephen Orgel. His essay offers wonderful opportunities for those who wish to explore the dramatic diversities of the eye and the ear. He sets up a fascinating play between the dramas of Inigo Jones and Ben Jonson, between the eye and the ear. Jonson saw the court masque as creating heroic roles for the leaders of society and teaching virtue in the most direct way, by example. The masque was put on as a corporate and festive identity and there tended to be no barrier between the audience and the actors. Orgel relates the spectacles provided by Jones's picturesque splendors ("nothing else but pictures with Light and Emotion") to "Renaissance psychological theory shared by both Aristotelians and Platonists." According to this theory, "The means of drama . . . was spectacle, its end was wonder, and the whole was an expression of the glory of princes." Orgel opens up the whole Baroque period with its sudden stress on spectacle and novelty of perspective that cause a violent encounter with the older verbal Establishment. The Baroque habit of polarized antithesis is richly illustrated in the conflict between the visual innovators and the oral poets and rhetoricians at Oxford in 1605 when a group of court officials arrived to check the arrangements at Christ Church. The bureaucrats, concerned for the King's image, protested that "the auditory could see but his cheek only." To the royal bureaucrats the spectators at a play were the "auditory" and the new illusionist art of perspective as practiced by Jones was wasted on them. While the masque used perspective art from 1605, "it was many years before the implications of this sort of theatre were realized in the drama, or indeed, recognized at all."

The implications of all this for architecture, and for painting, poetry, and sensibility are very great. The age was moving very rapidly to a conquest of the visual over the oral, but it was still centuries away from the ultimate Hollywood realization of this. By the time visual illusion had triumphed entirely, the oral returned via radio and talkies. Meanwhile, "the creation of exemplary roles for the leaders of the culture was one of the highest acts the Renaissance poet could perform," and is not unrelated to the twentieth-century "star system." Today, exemplary icons of the cultures of the world meet in prestigious rivalry and the warfare of the future may move more and more toward these "software" exercises and manoeuvres. As the masks of entire cultures are brought into play we may discover again what it means to "lose face" or identity itself. As societies once more become cohesive and corporate, the entire community can become an actor in a way that is normal in Oriental and non-Western societies in general. Western individualism, which allows an actor to take any part at any time, as if he were a substitute for the author's point of view, stands in contrast to the Kabuki theatre, for example. In this theatre, as in the NOH play, the audience as participants may go on the stage and offer the actor a cup of tea after a very long dialogue. The global theatre naturally uses the audience as cast, and "private citizens" could hardly be conceived to exist. Indeed, the scrubbing of private identity since TV leads naturally to the use of the out-of-doors and to institutional spaces as theatre, whether it be Woodstock or a student sit-in.

Apropos Ben Jonson's insistence that an imitation of an action is not the same as a mirror of man's life, Orgel stresses that "an imitation is an action and a mirror is not." However, under conditions of instant electric retrieval and replay the distinction between mirror and action may well get blurred. James Joyce pointed out that the mirror is a square wheel without spokes which is nourished by what it produces. The perpetual motion of the mirror is indeed an action that transcends even the forms of mass production which the Gutenberg press had initiated. The ultimate stage of mass production could thus become like the NOH play, not a mirror of reality but a play into a mirror.

If the contemporaries of Ben Jonson and Inigo Jones found perspective as difficult to adjust to as the 1920s found cubism, the sensibilities of the electronic era call for an even more arduous tuning in of perceptions. Sidney Homan's "When the Theatre

Turns to Itself" indicates just this kind of increase in self-consciousness of the theatrical medium. He approaches the theatre, that is to say, by its effects rather than its causes, a method of approach that Bernard Beckerman shares in his view that character is defined by his responses, by the resonance of his encounters.

Was it not the great innovation of the Symbolists that they suddenly turned away from cause and effect in order to look at the effects minus the causes? Accompanying this strategy was the discovery that there was a pattern in the effects which revealed the total process rather than an isolated cause. By turning to the medium itself, Homan is able to note the unique patterns of energy that it generates even in the crude Western theatre. He points to the pattern which Bogart fans have in their "repertory" sense of their idol in his successive film roles. He then reminds us how Shakespeare's audience would have related Burbage's roles in a similar way. But there is a further analogy or resonance within the individual play; for example, Hamlet encounters Claudius *visually* at his confessional and then is deceived once more by his eyes in Gertrude's chamber where he sees a figure moving behind the arras. Visual echoes of this kind are also central to the structure of *Othello*. In fact, it could be said that the entire symbolist awareness of the past century has been our awakening to the nature of the physical bond that is the space between situations. The play within the play of *Hamlet* reminds us that the magic of Ovid was omnipresent to the Elizabethans, as it was to Dante and Chaucer. The moment of metamorphosis is the moment of frustration, arrest, the hang-up. This moment can be realized dramatically in an [a]llusion, a parenthesis, an aside, or a sub-plot parallel to the larger action. The interface generated in these intervals is itself the occasion of metamorphosis and transformation of awareness.

Homan sees the greatness of the Renaissance theatre repeated in that of our own time:

> But this particular turning toward itself provides not just another instance of theatrical self-indulgence but easily Pirandello's most brilliant indictment of our common human dilemma. The difficulties of the stage, of communication, of separating pretense from sincerity, of "telling our story," become identical with those in life itself.

After the recent centuries of conceiving "truth" and "reality" as *matching* rather than *making*, Western man was not disposed to face the fact of faking as a legitimate feature of human consciousness. The students of James Joyce are familiar with the art process as inherent in the cognitive act of *making sense.*

The user of any medium or any technology is the content of that form. The reader is the content of any poem or of the language he employs, and in order to use any of these forms, he must put them on. The process of putting these on involves the reader in an imaginative exploration by which he discovers the possible extent and limitations of a medium. To the specialist or visual man, this put-on or play that is inherent in every moment of consciousness appears unreal, a sham. It is very easy for the Pirandellos or Genets to startle the literal-minded visual man with the evidence that his life is necessarily faking and making. In the magnetic city of the wired planet the world's population move instantly and *en masse* through all space, creating a new age of angelism, as it were. Now that we have all been translated into electric information, the imagination is no longer needed in order to people our world with beings and objects from everywhere at once. Thinking of these developments makes even Ionesco's stage seem trite and obvious. Homan turns to Beckett to illustrate the new self-consciousness of the stage as itself an actor. *Waiting for Godot* simply pulls the effect of waiting away from all the reasons for waiting, in literary symbolist style. The poetic fun is to restructure all the reasons from the mere effects.

Symbolism consists in pulling out connections; but connections are inevitably visual relations. One of the paradoxical effects of visual connectedness is the sub-division of human functions into jobs whereas when the visual connections are pulled out there is an immediate restoration of role-playing. The symbolists anticipated the effects of the new electric technology for their discontinuity created involvement and restored role-playing both for the artist and the citizen.

To enter the world of the Cherry Orchard of Chekhov through the portals of *Les Fleurs du Mal* is quite natural. Bernard Beckerman invites us to a structural analysis. The Russian world itself is symbolist to the extent that it cuts off the causes operative in the industrial revolution. The Russian culture appealed to the industrial age for reasons not unlike those which rendered the primitive world attractive to the 18th century. I would like to ask readers whether Ibsen's world, on the other hand, is not a kind of preview of the post-industrial world, just as Russia offers a romantic view of the pre-industrial world. Would it be true to suggest that Ibsen presents people minus community long before *The Waste Land*? The fragmented effects of industrial specialism inevitably erode communal realities. How did Ibsen's world achieve this advance status before industrialism arrived?

If some writers achieve an "advance status," there are others who cling to the past, who fear and resist the fragmented effect of the symbolist view. The resistance to the discontinuity of non-visual spaces can recall a hostility to change and a rage for a lost order. I confess I still respond with distaste to Yvor Winters's rationalist passion, explored by Jonas A. Barish in "Yvor Winters and the Antimimetic Prejudice." Years ago I wrote an essay on Winters entitled "Rhymer Reditus." Rhymer pushed the dying rhetorical doctrine of decorum to a frenetic pitch, classifying the performance of the poets according to their most literal relation to the styles indicated by their subjects. Winters pushed criticism into a pattern of concept minus percept, which was also an unwitting parody of paraphrase and poetic commentary of the preceding time. The great discovery of the Symbolists had been the need to start with effects even when dealing with ideas and systems. To perceive a theory or philosophy as itself an object for æsthetic experience and testing absolved poets and critics alike from any attempt to build a system. For Paul Valéry or Wallace Stevens, the making of such a system became observable as a poetic process of itself. One of the advantages of this existential approach is that banalities cease to trouble, since they can be elevated into an æsthetic of the absurd, as in the work of Flaubert. For the conceptual critic, untrained in the perceptual order of judgment and existence, the whole of art and life tend to be classified according to exclusive schemes of value. Thus for Winters "a poet imitating the thought processes of a character of smaller intelligence than his own, will inevitably... 'be writing poetry which as poetry will be of an inferior kind."

It is not necessary to say much more than that Winters was the uncritical victim of merely visual and written forms of literature. Winters "specifies a logical structure, or at least a paraphrasable content, as the essential basis of a good poem." The merely visual man, who holds all his other senses in abeyance, will naturally assume as a metaphor of any art form, that of a receptacle. Once this basis has been established, it is difficult to resist the need to use the receptacle as a waste basket. This is what Winters did. His "critical" activity thus consisted mainly in junking the classics by classification.

Every environment that we make and assume is a mask that can become a crushing weight distorting our sensibilities, unless countervailed by imaginative response. Winters was crushed by his mask, unlike Joyce, who was freed by his. "Yes, the viability of vicinals if invisible is invincible," Joyce wrote (*Finnegans Wake*, p. 81), alluding to the labyrinth of cognition. It is this sensory labyrinth that is limned as the very portrait of the artist on the opening page of the book of that name. The artist in us offers us freedom in the act of separating the experience from the objects that engender the experience. And this is the point Richard Courtney makes in "A Dramatic Theory of Imagination" that could be capsulated as "Man and His Masks."

Consider the mask of blindness in our visually-oriented Western world, as revealed in Jacques Lusseyran's *And There Was Light* (Boston, 1965). Blindness turned him into a seer able to perceive the multisensuous worlds concealed from the sighted:

When I came upon the myth of objectivity in certain modern thinkers it made me angry. So there was only one world for these people, the same for everyone. And all the other worlds were to be counted as illusions left over from the past. Or why not call them by their name—hallucinations? I had learned to my cost how wrong they were.

From my own experience I knew very well that it was enough to take from a man a memory here, an association there, to deprive him of hearing or sight, for the world to undergo immediate transformation, and for another world, entirely different but entirely coherent, to be born. Another world? Not really. The same world rather, but seen from another angle, and counted in entirely new measures. When this happened, all the hierarchies they called objective were turned upside down, scattered to the four winds, . . . (p. 112)

Obsession with the inner trip in our electric time is as compulsive as the Romantic obsession with outer trips and quests for the picturesque. The environmental mask that we now try to accommodate is no longer visual so much as audio-tactile, a fact recorded in the popularity of the terms "participative" and "involvement."

Courtney refers us to Piaget's analysis of the cognitive process of assimilation and accommodation: "Imitation is a continuation of assimilation, and intelligence a harmonious combination of the two." Perseverance is thus a primary component in imaginative intelligence.

My own concern with understanding the processes of man-made media finds much aid from Piaget. Since all media from speech to weapons, tools, and clothes are extensions of our own bodies, they also create new service environments or social masks of corporate power. In assimilating and accommodating these forms, whole populations imitate and play with them over long periods, nourishing their motives and values and re-forming their outlooks. The process Lusseyran describes in himself cannot but occur for large groups of people subjected to new masks of technological power.

My own study of these "masks" of power began with their effects rather than their causes, and I became aware that there was little recognition of the new patterns of energy generated by the arts of man. Puzzled by this gap in such basic study, I traced it back to the Greeks, who studied the entelechies or patterns of energy in nature, but not in human technologies. From Plato to the present, the Western world has ignored the entelechies, or psychic and social patterns of assimilation and accommodation, arising from such primary forms as writing or numbers. Lusseyran's blindness enabled him to see the strange bias of our philosophy for mere concept and classification, a bias that limited man's possibilities. Thus when Harold Innis began to detail the divergent political effects of writing on stone as opposed to paper, he was ignored. In *Empire and Communications* he explains how the Greeks destroyed their oral tradition and their culture with the new written forms. Innis did not have Piaget or Lusseyran to explain how the sensory assimilation of any new form may destroy earlier forms of sensory accommodation. More simply, inputs are never matched by outputs in cognition, whether private or corporate, and experience is not a repeat of sensation. Again, accommodation is a making, not a matching, process — a fact difficult of apprehension by the visually-oriented West, but easy for the Orient. The West readily accepts visual matching as a criterion of truth and science; and our ideas of "causation" have tended towards mere classification for 2500 years. To the Greek, for whom *phusis* or "nature" was a *figure* he had hoicked out of the *ground* of existence, it seemed that in creating the classification of phusis he had done all the entelechizing that was needed. Nature was his art form. The confusion of existence could be held at bay by this form, and human technologies were pushed beyond the range of philosophical study. "Nature" has thus been mask and performance for the West until the hydrogen bomb recalled us to the existential *ground*. Concern for *existenz* marks the end of many centuries of Nature. Yet Nature had been *imagined* by the Greeks by the action of internalizing the environmental forms arising from their assimilation and accommodation of the phonetic alphabet. Just how extreme an abstraction is represented by this alphabet can be gathered from a study reported in *Science* (March 26, 1971):

American Children with Reading Problems Can Easily Learn to Read English Represented by Chinese Characters

Abstract: With 2.5 to 5.5 hours of tutoring, eight second-grade inner city school children with clear reading disability were taught to read English material written as 30 different Chinese characters. This accomplishment eliminates certain general interpretations of dyslexia, for example, as a visual-auditory memory defecit. . . . It is proposed that much reading disability can be accounted for in terms of the highly abstract nature of the phoneme (the critical unit of speech in alphabetic systems) and that an intermediate unit, such as the syllable, might well be used to introduce reading.

Slow learners in the reading process were quickly upgraded by a course in the Chinese written character. Only students of high visual bias appear as superior in the Western world, and the slow learner is usually a multi-sensuous individual.

Courtney moves to the dramatic aspect of imagination via Piaget's notes on play: "The baby plays with a visual model in order to understand it, and then imitates its parts . . . ." The audile-tactile-kinetic-osmic spaces involved in a child's experience of any toy have parity with sight for the preliterate, yet we lump these together under the term "visual." Categories numb perception. Was it Piaget who told us that uttering, or the outering that is speech, begins when the child stops clutching its toys and begins to drop them? Courtney suggests that dramatic play begins with impersonation when a child is nearly a year old. It is an act of externalization of the internalized perceptions, that is, a kind of re-cognition, a re-play. Re-play may be a form of cognition; it is also a form of interpretation, a dramatic performance involving actors and audience.

Leonard B. Meyer's "Critical Analysis and Performance: The Theme of Mozart's A Major Piano Sonata" raises important questions about the judgment of performances. But it also leads to questions about seen and unseen audiences. Electric studio recordings have mostly eliminated the concert audience, while greatly enlarging the public for music. Glenn Gould is a performer whose observations on this matter have themselves been recorded with delightful illustrations. His contrast between performing for the man in the top gallery and for studio sound engineers comes through very well. As a technician, Gould feels far more affinity for the engineer than for a fashionable public that comes to the concert hall not so much to hear as to be seen. Gould's argument is, in part, that by eliminating the concert audience he can play for the composer. It may sound a little bit like Charles Lamb's expostulation: "Hang posterity, I'll write for the past."

Gould's meditations on changing relations of performer and audience, by means of the recording studio, give special point to Meyer's opening observations: "The performance of a piece of music is, therefore, the actualisation of an analytic act — even though such analysis may have been intuitive and unsystematic. For what a performer does is to make the relationships and patterns potential in the composer's score clear or unclear to the mind and ear of the experienced listener." He adds the remark of Edward Cone: "Active listening is, after all, a kind of vicarious performance . . . ." The question of the dramatic and mimetic presence of the performer is one that T. S. Eliot alludes to in "Portrait of a Lady":

> We have been, let us say, to hear the latest Pole
> Transmit the Preludes, through his hair and finger-tips.
> 'So intimate, this Chopin, that I think his soul
> Should be resurrected only among friends
> Some two or three, who will not touch the bloom
> That is rubbed and questioned in the concert room.'

How far Baroque music demanded the full attention of its auditory, and how far it tended to be an incidental background to ceremonious gatherings is not for me to say. However it is plain that recorded music can, on the one hand, be background to ordinary activities, or can, on the other hand, elicit intense attention.

The possibility of endless replay of compositions or passages has introduced an entirely new character into musical performance. Would not this fact tend to push music towards an extreme of self-conscious professionalism?

If music in the electronic age offers the possibility of endless replay, and replay may be a form of cognition and interpretation, is not portraiture — nude or clothed — governed by assumptions of role-playing?

The nude is in role. The naked person is like Lear, someone who has been dressed down and stripped of his role. The strip-teaser takes off her clothes in order to put on her audience. On stage she may be nude, but the moment she steps backstage she is naked. The audience is her mask. Recently, when a nude model in an art school fainted and fell from her chair, the students who had been drawing her proved unwilling to approach her to offer help or aid. She was naked from the moment that she fainted. She had slipped out of role. This does raise the question of whether the audience has a masculine or feminine relation to a performer. One can test this by the difficulties presented in staging a male strip-tease. Recently the wives of a men's club insisted that they have a male strip-teaser for a party at the club. The men, who had been in the habit of having female strippers, protested that a male strip-tease would degrade the club. They had raised not just a moral but an æsthetic and dramatic problem. Can a male strip-teaser be anything but a female impersonator? Is it possible for a female impersonator to do a male strip-tease? The answer is in the *effect* and opens up the problems of whether the audience as such has a masculine or feminine role. Is a member of any audience essentially female? Are the men at a ball game necessarily in a feminine posture of passivity? If rule is masculine, is the art of being ruled feminine? Are the passengers in an airplane in a feminine role? And are hijackers rapists?

Anne Hollander in "The Clothed Image: Picture and Performance" draws our attention to the fact that "dress has always been used to express variations of status, sexuality, wealth, age, reverence for supernatural power or simple whim." In *Finnegans Wake* the episode on the Prankquean presents dress as a piratical technology associated with weaponry and money and the rise of aggressive societies. Clothing as aggression and conquest over one's fellows and over nature appears in the aspect of the vortex; it constitutes a new flow of energy and power. This aggressive feature of clothing appears most obviously in the world of fashion. Anne Hollander comments on the *Nymph of the Spring* as having "her dress rolled up under her head for a pillow, and many such patently erotic figures have garments shown nearby, as if to stress just this sexual power in the relationship between fashionable clothing and desirable body."

Fashion is one of the most pervasive dramatic manifestations of our Western world and we may ask whether it is possible for fashion to exist in hieratic or stabilized role-playing societies. Fashion would seem to require a sudden new design for which there must be no apparent causes. The midi failed if only because its "motives" were all too obvious (the needs of the textile trade), whereas the mini had very hidden "causes," namely the hula-hoop and the twist that had preceded it. The hula-hoop was a manifestation of involvement very divergent from the old game of rolling a hoop on the ground. Moving inside a hula-hoop was itself a form of roll-playing, and the mini skirt is a tribal costume worn by both men and women in many societies. As such, the mini-skirt is not a fashion but a costume, and may prove to have great tenacity as "put on" in our electric time. Dress is private and individual, and one can "dress up" or "dress down," but costume is corporate putting on of a society itself. Anne Hollander reviews many features of the dressed image, whether in ecclesiastical vestment or in the classical draperies which became part of the stage properties of 18th century portraits. The Blue Boy of Gainsborough, for example, is not wearing clothes fashionable for his time, but an imitation of cavalier clothing of more than a century earlier. It is natural to speak of a "period costume" since it is not private but corporate dress.

It is the principal theme of *From Cliché to Archetype* that every innovation scraps its immediate predecessor while at the same time retrieving a much earlier form. The cavalier costume of *The Blue Boy* in the early industrial time is a small example of this, just as pre-Raphaelite ladies were simply unprecedented. Baudelaire began the symbolist inspection of contemporary effects in fashion and technology alike. It was a change of sensibility that quickly arrived at the Picabia technique of using water taps or carburetors as sitters for portraits. By simply abstracting the object from its supposed causes or uses and looking at it as if it were an archaeological survival, any artefact whatever becomes a fascinating art form. It was this awareness that led Baudelaire to deplore "the use of historical dress in academic paintings, calling it a form of laziness not to attempt to distill the beauty of contemporary fashion and make it eternal as did the great portrait artists of the past." Anne Hollander continues with his observations that when we ignore the esthetic lessons of modern fashion, "we cannot in fact recapture and convey the style of other days . . . ." Without sensibility and perceptions trained to find awareness in one's own time, one cannot really enter into other times. That the historical sense depends upon a full contemporary awareness has raised issues ever since for poets and scholars alike. The Symbolists had in fact, like Lewis Carroll, tuned into the electronic age whose instant character makes all times contemporary and the present historical. In an environment of instant information chronological history or visually organized time yields to ecological time and interplay of motives, for good or evil.

The corporate society as criminal or evil is precisely the subject of Ronald Sokol's essay on "The Political Trial: Courtroom as Stage, History as Critic." In the recent military trial of Lieutenant Calley the unfamiliar scope of public participation played strange tricks. When the audience of a trial includes an entire population or a nation, it is the public itself that appears as the criminal, and the culprit who appears a hero. May this not have happened with the trial and execution of Charles I? The sheer scale of the audience dwarfs the judicial establishment, transforming a political event into a dramatic action. It is an old observation of Aristotle and others that any process pushed to its limits reverses its characteristics. Thus, in the process of making and reporting "news," the scale of the services involved in gathering and projecting these items tends to exceed the events reported and "making the news" becomes of much greater consequence than the news itself. The news audience becomes the principal actor under these conditions, usurping the functions of the ordinary cast.

It is a matter that I question a good deal when trying to judge how much the Elizabethan theatre, for example, was "mounted" on the nascent public being formed by the printing press. I ask myself whether the writers for that press in the sixteenth century, at least, relied heavily on the conventional roles of medieval society as a means of relating themselves to their readers? By the same token, when the Reading Public was fully formed in the early eighteenth century the theatre switched from the traditional roles of medieval society to "realistic" representation. This raises the question whether the great age of the English, and indeed of the European, theatre was a transition from a society of role players to a society of work and jobs?

When Sokol refers to the trials of the McCarthy era, it is well to keep in mind that the public was putting on a totally new kind of mask, TV, just as the Elizabethan public began to look at the world through the mask of the printed page. This latter mask provided a unique innovation of precision and power, with the promise of unlimited repetition and vast performance. This is only one of the meanings of print, but it was not lost on Cervantes, or Rabelais, or Erasmus, or Aretino. Gigantism and ego-mania appear at once in the mask of the printed page. These aspects challenged Montaigne to a lifetime of interior analysis and self-portraiture even as they projected Don Quixote and the Conquistadores on to the stage of grandiose adventure. The mask of the printed page revealed the paradigms of precision and quantity to the new science, setting the stage for Galileo and the Royal Society alike.

By contrast the TV viewer of the McCarthy era had a totally unexpected performance presented to him. TV tore the newspaper mask off McCarthy and tossed him into the wastebasket. Unpredictably, TV reduced the dimensions of stars in the news to puny proportions and created the instant illusion of verisimilitude. "The Forsytes," as presented by the B.B.C., do not arouse the same controversial queries as arise in casting movie performers. The viewer is tempted to quarrel with the movie image of Cromwell, but the TV image of Cranmer or Wolsey tempts the viewer to say "I didn't realize they looked like that." That is, TV has much greater power to impose its assumptions than the movie does. As an entirely electric medium, TV also has much greater power to "transport" us and to transform our awareness. There is, as it were, an "angelic" dimension in electric media, lacking even to the movie.

When Sputnik went around the planet in 1957 the earth became enclosed in a man-made environment and became thereby an "art" form. The globe became a theatre enclosed in a proscenium arch of satellites. From that time the "audience" or the population of the planet became actors in a new sort of theatre. Mallarmé had thought that "the world exists to end in a book." It turned out otherwise. It has taken on the character of theatre or playhouse. Since Sputnik the entire world has become a single sound-light show. Even the business world has now taken over the concept of "performance" as a salient criterion.

Sokol comments on the role of public trials and witch-hunts in effecting the "expulsion of evils." The merely private citizen would scarcely seem adequate for this function in the global theatre. Whole cultures would now appear as necessary for arraignment in the age in which the Establishment itself has become the scapegoat. In the age of radio there had been a booze panic and prohibition, and the "demon rum" was harried and hunted. In the TV age of addiction to the inner trip, the drug panic has nominated a new villain. In the information environment of the "wired planet," man-hunting, with its multitudinous forms of espionage has become a universal drama.

What is the role of English study in this global theatre? In John Jordan's "Literary History at Berkeley" one finds a corporate profile or portrait that is fascinating, and *New Literary History* is successfully satisfying this need for a large gallery of similar departmental portraits as revealing the character of the unique vortices of power developed in the community of learning. The professional study of English as a university discipline is now in need of historical appraisal itself. Such study can increase the perceptual level not only of students of language and literature but can bring literary study into the full dialogue of contemporary culture. Even the most prosaic routines of instruction in one era can illuminate unheeded forms of study in another. Literary training in any period has features in common with the dominant forms of perception in all the other kinds of study. Do not the words of Sigfried Giedion relate to teachers of English as well as to the historian of technological change?

> For the historian there are no banal things. Like the scientist, the historian does not take anything for granted. He has to see objects not as they appear to the daily user, but as the inventor saw them when they first took shape. He needs the unworn eyes of contemporaries, to whom they appeared marvelous or frightening. At the same time, he has to establish their constellations before and after, and thus establish their meaning.

History writing is ever tied to the fragment. The known facts are often scattered broadcast, like stars across the firmament. It should not be assumed that they form a coherent body in the historical night. Consciously, then, we represent them as fragments, and do not hesitate, when necessary, to spring from one period to another. Pictures and words are but auxiliaries; the decisive step must be taken by the reader. In his mind the fragments of meaning here displayed should become alive in new and manifold relations. (*Mechanization Takes Command*, p. 3)

Literature has not always been the most privileged area of perception, yet the literary student can increase his awareness of language and the processes of expression from the whole life of his period, whether his stress be past or present. Accustomed to the study of individual and self-conscious *figures*, the literary student may easily ignore the anonymous and non-verbal *ground* of the culture that sustained the language and literature he takes for granted. In this perspective Professor Jordan's essay is very helpful. The first Chairman of the Berkeley English Department was William Swinton, appointed in 1868 to be "professor of the English Language and Literature, Rhetoric, Logic and History." That phrase alone tells of a long and complex development. It tells how the traditional verbal disciplines of the trivium were still central to the nascent and peripheral studies of English and History, and it also bespeaks the separation of verbal studies from the quadrivium of the sciences. "The Two Cultures" had already turned their backs on each other.

Swinton's historical survey course, despite many adventures, "has been with us always, and today it is the core of the English major." One might wish to discover at this point whether it was the new stress on the study of geography in the early nineteenth century that provided the paradigm and impulse for literary surveys? Was not Kant a founding father of modern geography? Did he not extend this study to mapping the interior regions of the human faculties? Are not humanist and language studies, quite as much as the sciences, subject to shaping by dominant tropes and paradigms of the society at large?

The power of the new outer "picturesque" landscape of the Romantics appeared in the nineteenth century as a means of organizing historical and literary study by sweeping panorama. Today, by contrast, a-historical literary study "in depth" suggests the new power of the inner landscape of the Symbolists. They had paralleled the discoveries of Claude Bernard in internal medicine — *le milieu intérieur*. No matter how the specialist of language or science strives to isolate his studies, he will find them resonating with the patterns and intensities of fields remote from his own. And is not the ground and existence of the common and shared measures of the language itself a main reason for this shared consciousness? Were not jazz and rock in the twenties and the fifties inseparable from the *ground* of spoken English? Is it possible to teach modern poetry without recognition of these dance-song forms that translate the sounds of the city into the rhythms of English?

It seems reasonable to assume, therefore, that students should be encouraged to see the *ground* of English itself as the necessary inspiration and nourishment of every aspect of the arts and science of their age. This issue of *New Literary History* exploring "performances" reveals that literature can indeed provide insights into a multi-cognitive, multi-sensuous world. Being myself a professor of English, I see that assuming the role of a "stranger" provoking a dialogue has been an incitement to global thinking. Although I began with one role, I have played many parts in this "Commentary." The "stranger" has become the guide; the passenger, the driver. Since this multi-role-playing is inevitable in an electronic world, one hopes that the put-on has also been a turn-on.

Roles, Masks and Performances
Marshall McLuhan - Unbound (12)

ISBN: 1-58423-051-7
Library of Congress Control Number 2005927213

Marshall McLuhan Unbound Project Editors
Eric McLuhan, W. Terrence Gordon

Published in United States in October 2005 by
Gingko Press, Inc.
5768 Paradise Drive, Suite J · Corte Madera, CA 94925
(415) 924-9615 · Fax (415) 924-9608
email: books@gingkopress.com
http://www.gingkopress.com

Design, packaging and production: Die Gestalten Verlag, Berlin
Layout and Typography: onlab, Berlin
Fonts: *Dolly* by Underware, *Bullet* by House Industries
Production: Martin Bretschneider, Vinzenz Geppert
Art direction: Robert Klanten

Made in Germany